WESTERN
RECIPES

Amie Jane Leavitt

Mitchell Lane
PUBLISHERS

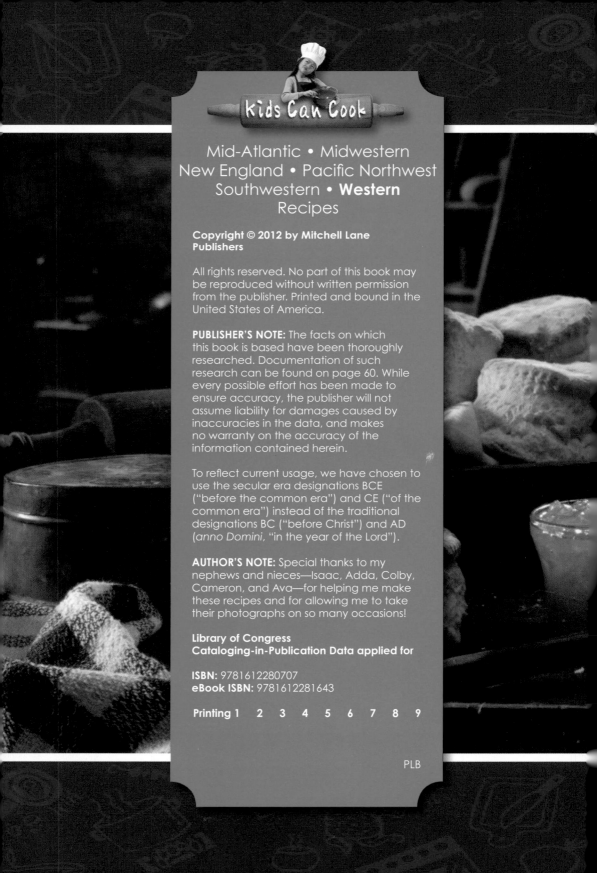

Kids Can Cook

Mid-Atlantic • Midwestern
New England • Pacific Northwest
Southwestern • **Western**
Recipes

Copyright © 2012 by Mitchell Lane Publishers

PUBLISHER'S NOTE: The facts on which this book is based have been thoroughly researched. Documentation of such research can be found on page 60. While every possible effort has been made to ensure accuracy, the publisher will not assume liability for damages caused by inaccuracies in the data, and makes no warranty on the accuracy of the information contained herein.

To reflect current usage, we have chosen to use the secular era designations BCE ("before the common era") and CE ("of the common era") instead of the traditional designations BC ("before Christ") and AD (*anno Domini*, "in the year of the Lord").

AUTHOR'S NOTE: Special thanks to my nephews and nieces—Isaac, Adda, Colby, Cameron, and Ava—for helping me make these recipes and for allowing me to take their photographs on so many occasions!

**Library of Congress
Cataloging-in-Publication Data applied for**

ISBN: 9781612280707
eBook ISBN: 9781612281643

Printing 1   2   3   4   5   6   7   8   9

PLB

THE MENU

INTRODUCTION

The American West is a vast area that is made up of the following states: Colorado, Wyoming, Montana, Idaho, Utah, New Mexico, Arizona, Nevada, Washington, Oregon, California, Alaska, and Hawaii. This book focuses on foods from northern California, Nevada, Utah, Colorado, and Hawaii.

The food in the West has had many influences. The land—from the cattle-producing range to the fertile San Joaquin Valley—and the sea (the Pacific Ocean) have provided such fresh food dishes as Peach Cobbler and West Coast Fish Cakes.

When the Spaniards established Catholic missions during the 1500s, the combination of Spanish and Native American cultures produced new fare. Modern recipes such as Taco Ranch Casserole, Fish Tacos, and Taquitos are a result of that influence.

By the early 1800s, mountain men and cowboys from the East were trapping, hunting, exploring, and riding the range across this vast region. Pioneers traveled by covered wagon from the East to start a new life in the untamed Western wilderness. These European Americans and many Native American groups lived a life on the move. Their food included ingredients that they could easily transport and cook over a campfire. The dishes they made were generally hearty and rustic. Pioneer Biscuits, Utah Scones, Chuck Wagon Baked Beans, Santa

Maria Style Barbecue, and various versions of chili are part of this heritage.

When people flooded to California during the gold rush of 1849, they brought bread starters with them to make baking easier. From these starters came the famous San Francisco sourdough bread. Around the same time, thousands of Asians began immigrating from across the Pacific Ocean to work on the Transcontinental Railroad. They brought their own dishes, and Asian eateries cropped up all across the West. Their recipes also became part of Western cuisine, including sushi, made by wrapping rice and dried seaweed around vegetables or seafood. From this tradition the California Roll was born.

During the 1940s and 1950s, a number of restaurants that are now global phenomena got their start in the West. In 1946 in San Bernardino, California, World War II veteran Glen Bell opened a fast-food restaurant he called Taco Bell. Two years later in the same town, Dick and Mac McDonald started a small hamburger shop, which they named McDonald's. Then, in 1951 in San Diego, Robert O. Peterson opened the first Jack in the Box restaurant, featuring sandwiches made on sourdough bread. These restaurants continue to thrive, earning billions of dollars in worldwide markets. Other restaurants invented entirely new dishes, such as Fry Sauce and the French-Dipped Sandwich, that later swept the nation.

During the 1970s, many Westerners, especially those in California, began adopting a healthier lifestyle. They ate more fresh vegetables and whole grains; and less meat, sugars, and processed foods. A blend of cuisines called fusion cooking caught on, and when California chefs simplified their methods and added local fresh vegetables, they found they had invented California cuisine. California-style Pizza and Grilled Veggie Sandwiches became popular menu items.

Even with all these changes in cooking styles, much of the food of the American West harks back to Wild West days. We hope you enjoy making and eating these dishes as much as we do!

Kitchen Safety

For successful cooking, be sure to read the recipe all the way through before you start. Assemble the ingredients and tools you'll need before you begin, and your projects will be much more fun.

Make certain your hair is tied back, your sleeves are rolled up for most cooking but down when frying, and your hands are washed. Wear oven mitts when handling anything hot. Stoves, ovens, grills, and sharp items, such as knives and graters, should be used only under **adult** supervision.

Chuck Wagon Baked Beans

In the Old West, cowboys and pioneers had to eat foods that they could haul with them on horseback or in their wagons. Dried pinto beans were light. They were also easy to cook. Many evening meals included pinto beans cooked in kettles or Dutch ovens in roaring campfires.

There are many different ways to cook pinto beans. This tasty recipe doesn't need a campfire—it can be made in a regular oven.

Preparation Time: 15 to 20 minutes
Cooking Time: 3½ hours
Serves: 8 to 10

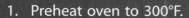

Ingredients

2 30-ounce cans pork & beans (or use vegetarian beans)
1 cup brown sugar
1 large green pepper, chopped
1 large onion, chopped
8 ounces crushed pineapple, drained
1¼ cups ketchup
1½ tablespoons Worcestershire sauce

1. Preheat oven to 300°F.
2. Mix all the ingredients together, then pour them into a 9 x 13-inch casserole dish.
3. Bake for 3½ hours.

Dutch Oven-style Potatoes

A Dutch oven is a cast-iron pot with a lid that can be used right in campfires to cook food. These pots are still used for camping, but usually not for everyday cooking. A popular breakfast item to cook in a Dutch oven is potatoes. These potatoes taste similar to Dutch oven potatoes, but you can make them in the kitchen by using a skillet on your stovetop.

Preparation Time: 15 to 20 minutes
Cooking Time: 20 to 30 minutes
Serves: 4 to 6

Ingredients

4 potatoes, peeled and diced
1 onion, peeled and diced
2 tablespoons butter
Salt
Pepper

1. Melt the butter in a skillet over low heat.
2. Add the potatoes and onions. Cook on medium heat, stirring constantly, until the onions are clear and potatoes are golden. You might need to add a bit more butter as you go.
3. Add salt and pepper to taste.

Sour Cream Potatoes

Like their European ancestors, the pioneers found many uses for cream that, without refrigeration, turned sour. In the West, sour cream potatoes are a popular side dish to bring to large gatherings. They are frequently included in menus for Christmas Eve dinners, wedding brunches, family reunion potlucks, and other special get-togethers.

Preparation Time: 10 minutes
Cooking Time: 30 minutes
Serves: 10

Ingredients

1 package (2 pounds) frozen shredded hash browns
½ cup + 2 tablespoons butter, melted
1 pint sour cream
1 can (10 ounces) cream of chicken soup
1 cup grated cheddar cheese
½ cup green onions, cut small
1 cup corn flakes or crisped rice cereal

1. Preheat oven to 350°F.
2. Pour frozen hash browns into a large mixing bowl. Add ½ cup melted butter, sour cream, soup, cheese, and onions. Mix well.
3. Spread this mixture into a greased 9 x 13-inch baking pan.
4. In a small bowl, mix cereal and 2 tablespoons melted butter.
5. Sprinkle this mixture on top of the potato casserole.
6. Bake for 30 minutes.

Old West Hamburger Soup

On a cold day in the West, a hearty bowl of soup is the perfect idea for dinner. This soup is filled with plenty of ingredients that a person could have grown in a garden and then stored for the winter, including potatoes, carrots, celery, and tomatoes. If your family limits foods with red meat, you can substitute ground turkey for the ground beef.

Preparation Time: 20 to 25 minutes
Cooking Time: 2 hours
Serves: 6

Ingredients

1 pound ground beef
3 teaspoons salt
½ teaspoon pepper
1 large onion, chopped
¾ cup mixed vegetable
   juice
¾ cup barley
½ cup uncooked rice
2 tablespoons dried parsley
1 quart canned tomatoes
2 quarts water
3 carrots, diced, or a dozen baby carrots
2 stalks celery, diced
3 potatoes, cubed
½ cup sugar (less, if desired)
1 teaspoon Worcestershire sauce

1. In a soup pot, brown the ground beef. Drain the fat.
2. Add salt and pepper.

BARLEY

3. Add onions. Cook until tender.
4. Add the rest of the ingredients. Bring to a boil.
5. Lower heat. Let soup simmer for 2 hours. Cooking it this long will make the soup creamy, as the rice and barley will fall apart.

Hawaiian Plate Lunch Salad

A traditional lunch in Hawaii doesn't include a sandwich and chips. Instead, people pack meat and side dishes such as rice and macaroni salad. Although Hawaii has been a state only since 1959, these "plate lunches" have been around since the 1880s. In those days, many Asian immigrants worked on sugar and pineapple plantations in Hawaii. They would bring a boxed lunch that was made up of leftovers from the previous night's dinner. Today, plate lunches are still very popular in Hawaii.

The base for a plate lunch salad is just macaroni and mayonnaise—up to two and a half cups of mayo for each pound of macaroni. You can eat it this way, or you can add other textures and flavors with a variety of vegetables and "leftovers."

Preparation Time: 10 minutes
Cooking Time: 10 to 15 minutes + 5 hours in the refrigerator
Serves: 6 to 8

Ingredients

1 pound elbow macaroni
¼ cup grated onion
3 heaping spoonfuls mayonnaise (up to 2½ cups; to taste)
Salt and pepper
Ideas for optional add-ins: tuna fish, chopped shrimp, or chopped ham; smashed hard-boiled eggs; grated carrots; chopped celery; thawed frozen peas

1. Cook the macaroni according to package directions, but add a minute or two to the longest cooking time so that they become very soft. Drain.
2. Pour the hot noodles into a mixing bowl. Add onion, mayonnaise, salt, and pepper. Mix well.
3. Add any other ingredients you'd like and stir gently. Add more mayonnaise if needed.
4. Refrigerate for at least 5 hours or until very cold. If the macaroni has absorbed most of the mayonnaise, add more to taste. The salad should be coated and creamy but not runny.

Cobb Salad

Avocados are native to southwestern Mexico, but they have been grown north of there for centuries. They grow well in the western United States, where they are very popular. This creamy fruit can be mashed to make a spicy dip called guacamole, cubed on crackers or hot toast, and sliced into salads. In fact, in 1937, Bob Cobb, who owned a Hollywood restaurant called The Brown Derby, invented the Cobb salad when he threw together avocados and other ingredients he simply had handy in the fridge.

Preparation Time: 15 minutes
Serves: 4

Ingredients

1 head of romaine lettuce or 1 bag of mixed greens
1 bunch green onions (scallions), chopped
4 chicken breasts, cooked and diced
2 hard-boiled eggs, chopped
1 large tomato, seeded and chopped
$1/2$ pound bacon, cooked and broken into pieces
2 ripe avocados, chopped
$1/4$ to $1/2$ cup crumbled blue cheese

Dressing
$2/3$ cup vegetable oil
$1/4$ cup limejuice
2 tablespoons sugar
2 tablespoons orange juice
1 teaspoon grated orange peel
1 teaspoon grated lime peel

1. Toss lettuce with green onions and dressing. Divide into four equal portions.
2. Top each portion with chicken, egg, tomato, bacon, avocado, and blue cheese. Serve immediately.

Cowboy Skillet Breakfast

After waking up early to do chores, cowboys and farm workers in the West often come back to the house to have a big hearty breakfast of eggs and potatoes with a side of bacon, ham, or sausage. This recipe combines all of these ingredients into one dish. Remember, it doesn't have to be made just for breakfast. It makes a great dinner, too.

Preparation Time: 15 minutes
Cooking Time: 15 to 20 minutes
Serves: 4 to 6

Ingredients

8 eggs
½ cup milk
½ cup cheddar cheese, grated
½ tablespoon butter
2 cups frozen hash browns or southern cubed potatoes
1 cup chopped ham
Salt
Pepper

1. Use a wire whisk to beat the eggs and milk until the mixture is foamy.
2. Mix in the cheese.
3. Melt the butter in a skillet over low heat.
4. Add the potatoes and ham to the pan. Cook over medium heat until the ham is crispy and the potatoes are golden brown.
5. Reduce the heat to low. Add the egg-and-cheese mixture. Cook, stirring constantly, until the eggs are thoroughly cooked.

Grilled Veggie Sandwich
on Sourdough Bread

Bread is made using some type of active ingredient (such as yeast) that makes the dough rise. Back in the 1800s when people were settling the West, pioneers would keep a small portion of dough from each of their batches. They used this dough to "start" the next batch. The starters in San Francisco began to have an unusual sour taste—the starter hadn't spoiled, and in fact the flavorful bread became popular. More and more people sought out the sour starter, and the sourdough bread of San Francisco became famous.

Since many people in this particular area also enjoy a vegetarian lifestyle (a diet without meat), here is a dish that combines a taste of the Old West with a taste of the new.

Preparation Time: 20 minutes
Cooking Time: 30 minutes
Serves: 4

Ingredients

¼ cup mayonnaise
3 cloves garlic, minced
1 tablespoon lemon juice
1 cup red bell peppers, sliced
1 small zucchini, sliced
1 red onion, sliced
1 small yellow squash, sliced
2 tablespoons olive oil
8 slices sourdough bread
½ cup feta cheese

1. If you will be using wooden skewers to cook the vegetables, soak the skewers in water for 10 minutes.
2. Meanwhile, mix the mayonnaise, garlic, and lemon juice in a bowl. Let it rest in the refrigerator.

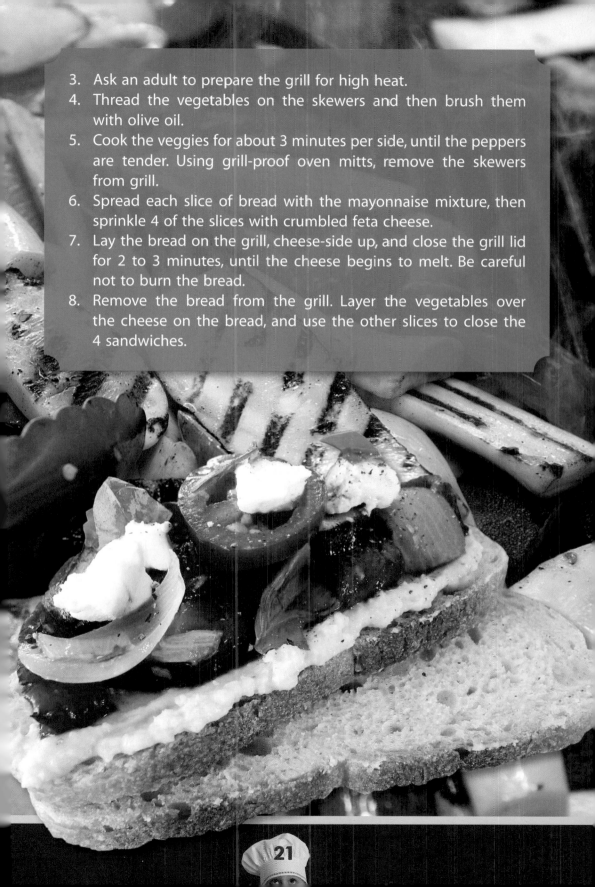

3. Ask an adult to prepare the grill for high heat.
4. Thread the vegetables on the skewers and then brush them with olive oil.
5. Cook the veggies for about 3 minutes per side, until the peppers are tender. Using grill-proof oven mitts, remove the skewers from grill.
6. Spread each slice of bread with the mayonnaise mixture, then sprinkle 4 of the slices with crumbled feta cheese.
7. Lay the bread on the grill, cheese-side up, and close the grill lid for 2 to 3 minutes, until the cheese begins to melt. Be careful not to burn the bread.
8. Remove the bread from the grill. Layer the vegetables over the cheese on the bread, and use the other slices to close the 4 sandwiches.

California Roll

During the 1800s, many people from Asian countries started immigrating to the West Coast of the United States. They came for work, mainly to help build the railroads. They brought some of their traditional foods with them, including sushi from Japan. The California roll—an offspring of sushi—became popular in the 1970s. Although some California roll recipes call for crabmeat along with rice, avocados, and cucumbers, this one is strictly vegetarian. You can find the Japanese ingredients, including the nori, wasabi, and other sauces, in the Asian section of most large grocery stores, in health food stores, and in Asian markets.

Cooking Time: 10 minutes
Preparation Time: 30
    minutes
Serves: 6 to 8 (makes
    about 50 pieces)

Ingredients

- 10 sheets (1 package) nori (roasted seaweed)
- 4 cups sushi rice (or substitute sticky brown rice)
- Japanese rice wine vinegar
- 4 to 6 tablespoons sugar
- 1 cucumber, peeled, seeded, and cut lengthwise into thin strips
- 3 carrots, cut lengthwise into thin strips
- 2 avocados, peeled and sliced lengthwise into thin strips
- Plum sauce
- Wasabi paste (careful not to use too much—it's really spicy!)
- Pickled ginger
- Soy sauce

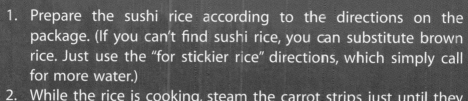

1. Prepare the sushi rice according to the directions on the package. (If you can't find sushi rice, you can substitute brown rice. Just use the "for stickier rice" directions, which simply call for more water.)
2. While the rice is cooking, steam the carrot strips just until they are limp (but still crunchy).
3. In a large bowl, mix the rice vinegar and sugar. It should be sour—not enough to make you pucker—and just a little bit sweet.
4. Pour the cooked rice into the bowl with the sugar and vinegar. Mix it around for a couple of minutes until the rice cools down a bit.

5. Spread a sheet of nori on a sushi rolling mat. (If you don't have a rolling mat, you can use a plastic placemat or even strong plastic wrap.) Using the back of a wet spoon, spread the rice on the nori, leaving a strip about 2 inches wide along one edge. The rice layer should be about ½ inch thick.

6. Spread a thin layer of plum sauce over the rice.

7. Lay 1 to 2 slices each of the cucumber, carrots, and avocado. Line them up next to each other, and make sure the line of each type of vegetable goes all the way across the rice. (The pieces should be parallel to the bare strip of nori.)

8. Using your mat or mat substitute, roll the vegetables up in the nori, just as you would roll up a sleeping bag. Press down as you go to keep the roll tight.

9. Place the roll seam-side down on a cutting board and let it rest. The rice will steam the bare strip of nori, sealing the roll.

10. Using a damp knife, cut each roll into bite-sized pennies, about 1½ inches wide. Wipe the knife between making each slice; otherwise, the rice will stick to the knife and tear the nori.

11. Serve with wasabi, pickled ginger, and soy sauce.

Santa Maria Style Barbecue

It seems that every region of the country has its own way of making barbecue. The way they make it in Santa Maria, California, started in the mid 1800s. Ranchers used special cuts of meat—called top-block sirloin—and rolled them in a mixture of salt and other seasonings. They smoked the meat over coals of red oak, a type of tree that is native to the Santa Maria Valley, and served them to their cowboys, called vaqueros. Now people come from far and wide to sample Santa Maria Style Barbecue, served with tiny pink beans called pinquitos, which also originated in this valley; homemade salsa; French bread; green salad; and strawberry shortcake.

You can re-create this cowboy barbecue at home using tri-tip roasts, which have also become a mainstay in this style of barbecuing. You can purchase red oak chips online, or you can use other hardwood chips such as mesquite to get a real smoky flavor from your barbecue grill. (The more wood you use, the more smoke you will get.) You will definitely need to work with an adult for this recipe. Serve it with a favorite side—french fries with a Western condiment called Fry Sauce.

Preparation Time: 40 minutes
Cooking Time: 45 to 60 minutes
Serves: 8

Ingredients

2 teaspoons black pepper
2 teaspoons cayenne pepper
4 tablespoons garlic powder
6 tablespoons salt
2 tri-tip roasts, 3 pounds each
Red oak wood chips

1. With an adult's help, trim the fat from the tri-tips. Leave only a thin layer of fat on one side.
2. Mix together the first four ingredients, called seasoning salt, in a small bowl.
3. Rub both sides of the meat with the seasoning salt. Let the meat sit in a shallow pan for 30 minutes.
4. Meanwhile, soak the wood chips in a bowl of water.
5. Heat an outdoor grill to low. Add the wood chips. Adjust the grate to the highest setting.
6. Place the meat on the grill, fat side up. Cook until this side gets crispy—about 15 minutes—then turn the meat over and cook it for another 15 minutes.
7. Turn the meat back over to the first side and cook for about 10 more minutes. You will notice the meat beginning to swell—this is what you want it to do. Don't poke it or try to flatten it.
8. Turn it one more time to finish cooking on the second side. Professional barbecue chefs recommend cooking this meat just until medium rare.
9. Remove the meat from heat and cover it loosely with foil. Let the meat rest for 10 to 15 minutes.
10. Slice across the grain and at an angle, about a half inch thick.

Fry Sauce

In the 1940s in Utah, Chef Don Carlos Edwards introduced a new condiment to use with french fries. When Don Carlos Barbecue became a fast-food restaurant called Arctic Circle, the concoction came to be called pink sauce or fry sauce. Customers loved it immediately, and it has been popular in this part of the West (mainly Utah and Idaho) ever since. Today, if you order fries at any restaurant in these two states, you will be asked if you want ketchup or fry sauce to go with them. To make this condiment at home, just mix equal parts of ketchup (or barbecue sauce) and mayonnaise.

French-Dipped Sandwich

The French-Dipped Sandwich consists of a long hoagie bun stuffed with thinly sliced roast beef and served with a side of beef broth called au jus ("with juice"), in which you dip the sandwich before you eat it. Two restaurants in California, Philippe's and Cole's, each claim to have invented these juicy sandwiches in the early 1900s—and the restaurants remain in friendly competition over which one makes the best dips. Regardless of who thought of the idea first, the French-Dipped Sandwich has become popular not only in the region but also throughout the United States.

Preparation time: 45 minutes
Cooking time: 45 to 60 minutes
Serves: 8 to 12 (makes 16 sandwich halves)

Ingredients

1 (4-pound) beef roast, either rib eye, sirloin, or tenderloin
½ cup coarse-ground black pepper
Dipping Sauce (see page 29)
8 French-bread rolls
Butter

1. Preheat oven to 425°F.
2. Place beef roast onto a rack in a shallow baking pan. Sprinkle pepper over roast, and, with clean, dry hands, press the pepper into the meat.
3. Bake, uncovered, 30 to 45 minutes. The meat is done when a thermometer in the thickest part of roast registers 135°F.
4. Ask an adult to take the roast out of the oven and transfer it to a cutting board. Pour the juice from the roasting pan into a medium saucepan.
5. Cover the beef loosely with foil and let it rest for 15 minutes. Meanwhile, prepare Dipping Sauce.
6. Ask the adult to carve the beef into thin slices.

Dipping Sauce
Drippings from roasting pan
1 can (10.5 ounces) beef broth
½ cup water
Salt and pepper to taste

To the saucepan of beef drippings (from step 4), add the other sauce ingredients. Bring the mixture to a boil, stir, then turn off the heat. Cover the pan and let it sit for 10 minutes.

7. For each sandwich: Cut the rolls in half. Butter the cut sides of each roll and toast (use a toaster oven or ask an adult to place them on a baking sheet under the broiler).
8. Layer about ½ pound of sliced beef on the bottom of each roll; add the top of the roll to each sandwich. Cut the sandwiches in half and serve each one with mustard and a small bowl of hot Dipping Sauce. (Each person should have his or her own bowl of sauce, because everyone will want to double dip!)

California-style Pizza

Pizza out West is not like pizza in other parts of the country. For one thing, in the West, the crust is allowed to rise after it is spread on the pan; and it is sometimes baked before the toppings are added to help keep it airy. The most important difference, though, is the toppings, which can range from exotic vegetables such as asparagus and squash to meats such as smoked salmon, barbecued chicken, and Peking duck. The sauce may be Italian-style pizza sauce, but often other sauces are used, such as mole on Mexican pizza. Here's a recipe for California-style pizza with barbecued chicken.

Preparation Time: 15 minutes
Cooking Time: 15 to 18 minutes
Serves: 2

Ingredients

¾ pound boneless skinless chicken breasts, diced
1 green pepper, cut into thin strips
¼ cup thin red onion slices
1 ready-to-use baked pizza crust, plain or whole wheat (12-inch)
⅓ cup barbecue sauce, as spicy as you like it
1½ cups shredded cheddar cheese blend

1. Preheat oven to 400°F.
2. Spray a large skillet with cooking spray. Over medium heat, cook chicken and vegetables for 4 to 5 minutes until chicken is done (it should no longer be pink).
3. Spread barbecue sauce over the pizza crust.
4. Top with chicken mixture and then cheeses.
5. Place pizza directly on middle oven rack. Bake 15 to 18 minutes or until crust is crispy and cheese is melted.

Fish Tacos

In California, Mexican food is particularly popular. Since California has a long coastline, seafood is also very popular in this state—so it's no surprise that many people love dishes like fish tacos. This version is super easy because it calls for fish sticks. You might also like to try making them using the West Coast Fish Cakes on the next page.

Preparation Time: 20 minutes
Cooking Time: 1 to 2 minutes
Serves: 2

Ingredients

6 fish sticks, cooked
    according to package directions
2 corn tortillas, warmed in microwave
Grated cheese
Lettuce
Avocados
Any other ingredients you like
    on tacos, such as sour cream,
    olives, tomatoes, and salsa

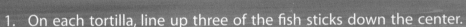

1. On each tortilla, line up three of the fish sticks down the center.
2. Top the fish with cheese, lettuce, avocado slices, and any other toppings you like.

West Coast Fish Cakes

On the East Coast, many people love eating crab cakes. They're popular in the West, too—but we often use different kinds of fish in our cakes, such as tuna or salmon.

These can be served plain and eaten with your hands or with a fork. If you'd like to make them into a meal, you can serve them on a roll or bun and top them with mayo, pickles, lettuce, and cheese. You could also use them to make Fish Tacos.

Preparation Time: 10 minutes
Cooking Time: 5 to 8 minutes
Serves: 10

Ingredients

1 cup milk
2 cups crushed
   saltine crackers
1 egg
2 tablespoons
   dried onions, or
   1 small onion,
   chopped
1 can (7 to 12 ounces) of
   your favorite type of fish (such
   as tuna, salmon, or crabmeat), drained
2 tablespoons butter

1. Place first 5 ingredients together in a bowl and mix thoroughly with a fork.
2. Form mixture into 8 palm-size cakes.
3. Melt the butter in a frying pan on the stove. Turn the heat to medium, then gently place the cakes in the pan.
4. Fry the cakes on this side until golden brown, then turn them over and fry them on the other side.

Taquitos

A creative California cook turned traditional Mexican flautas ("flutes") into taquitos ("little tacos"). Legend has it that Ralph Pesqueria invented taquitos at the El Indio Restaurant in San Diego in 1940. Both taquitos and flautas are made by rolling a tortilla tightly around shredded spiced beef, pork, or chicken and then deep-frying it.

This recipe shows you how to make cheese-and-chicken taquitos. If you'd rather not deep-fry these, you can bake them at 400°F for 6 to 8 minutes or until the tortillas are crisp and the filling is hot. Of course, you can modify the recipe further and just use cheese and beans, Halloween Chili (see page 56), or any other filling you'd like. Whatever you choose, you'll need about 2 cups of filling for 12 tortillas.

Preparation Time: 10 minutes
Cooking Time: 15 minutes
Serves: 4

Ingredients

1 cup chicken breast meat, cooked and shredded
⅓ cup green salsa
1 cup shredded cheese
12 corn tortillas

1. Heat oil in a deep-fryer to 350°F.
2. Mix the chicken, salsa, and cheese in a small bowl.
3. Warm the tortillas in a microwave, then spoon the filling down the center of each one (about 2 tablespoons in each). Leave a little room at each end so that filling does not fall out.
4. Roll the tortillas tightly and fasten with toothpicks. Each taquito should be only about an inch and a half wide.
5. With an adult, fry them in batches of 4 for about 3 to 5 minutes each. They should float, and then turn golden brown. Drain on paper towels.
6. Remove the toothpicks and serve.

Flautas and taquitos are so similar that in some places, both names are used for the same thing.

Taco Ranch Casserole

Tacos and ranch dressing are both very popular food items in the West. It makes sense, then, to combine them in the same dish for dinner.

Preparation Time: 20 to 25 minutes
Cooking Time: 20 to 30 minutes
Serves: 6 to 8

Ingredients

1 pound ground beef or turkey
1 can (8 ounces) tomato sauce
½ package taco or enchilada seasoning
1 can condensed cream of mushroom soup
½ cup ranch dressing
10 corn tortillas, cut in half
2 cups shredded cheese
Cooking spray

1. Preheat oven to 350°F.
2. In a skillet over medium heat, brown the meat.
3. Drain off any grease.
4. Add tomato sauce and seasoning. Simmer on low heat.
5. In a separate bowl, mix mushroom soup and ranch dressing together.
6. Mist cooking spray in a 9 x 13-inch dish. Pour in half the meat mixture.
7. Lay half of the tortilla pieces over the meat mixture.
8. Top this with half of the soup mixture.
9. Top the soup mixture with half of the cheese.
10. Repeat the layers in the same order as steps 6–9.
11. Bake for 20 to 30 minutes.

Indoor Cookout:
Sleeping Bag Hotdogs

There's nothing quite like roasting hot dogs and marshmallows over an open campfire on a warm summer evening. However, it doesn't have to be summertime for you to enjoy the taste of roasted hot dogs. You can eat them any time of the year if you're willing to cook them in an oven. This recipe shows you how to make a special kind of roasted hot dog: one that is wrapped in a bread-dough sleeping bag!

Preparation Time: 10 minutes
Cooking Time: 15 to 18 minutes
Serves: 12

Ingredients

12 hotdogs
1 11-ounce can of refrigerator breadsticks

1. Preheat oven to 350°F.
2. Lay the breadstick strips on a cutting board. Use a butter knife to cut each breadstick strip in half lengthwise.
3. Pick up one hot dog and one breadstick strip. Start at one end of the hot dog and wrap the dough around it until the entire dog is covered. Do this with all the dogs.
4. Place the wrapped dogs on a cookie sheet. Bake for 15 to 18 minutes or until the sleeping bag dough is golden brown.

Pioneer Biscuits

Biscuits were a popular bread item for pioneers to make. They required few ingredients and could be made quickly before a meal—unlike yeast bread or sourdough bread, which required time to rise before they could be baked.

Preparation Time: 15 to 20 minutes
Cooking Time: 8 to 10 minutes
Makes: 12 biscuits

Ingredients

2 cups flour
4 teaspoons baking powder
3 teaspoons sugar
½ teaspoon salt
½ cup cold butter
1 egg
⅔ cup cold milk
Butter

1. Preheat the oven to 450°F.
2. In a small bowl, mix the flour, baking powder, sugar, and salt.
3. Using two forks or a pastry blender, cut in the butter until the mixture resembles coarse crumbs.
4. In a measuring cup, beat the egg with milk.
5. Stir the milk mixture into the dry ingredients until just moistened. Do not mix too long; the less you mix biscuits, the better.
6. Lightly flour a large cutting board and place the dough onto the board.
7. Knead with your hands 20 times. Be sure to count. More than 20 and your biscuits will be tough instead of flaky.
8. Press the dough out on the board until it is about ¾ inch thick.
9. Cut circles in the dough using a biscuit cutter or a cup that is about 2½ inches wide.

10. Place the circles close together on a lightly greased pan.
11. Bake for 8 to 10 minutes until golden brown.
12. When you take the pan out of the oven, place a small pat of butter on top of each biscuit.

Utah Scones with Honey Butter

Every spring, the fourth graders in my elementary school enjoyed holding a Mountain Man Rendezvous. It commemorated a year spent learning about Western history. Utah scones with honey butter were always a hit at the event.

Utah scones, or fry bread, are a traditional Native American food. Each family or clan had its own recipe for this staple dish. The mountain men and pioneers who associated with the Native Americans adopted this tasty bread into their diets, too, and added toppings such as honey, jam, and honey butter. Topped with Halloween Chili (see page 56), sour cream, lettuce, and salsa, they make Navajo Tacos.

Kids can prepare these on their own, but they will need an adult to help fry the scones in the hot oil.

Preparation Time: 1½ hours, including rising time
Cooking Time: 20 minutes
Serves: 8 to 10

Ingredients

1 tablespoon yeast
1 cup warm water
½ cup sugar
1 cup milk, scalded
1 cup mashed potatoes,
    instant or real
¾ cup shortening
2 teaspoons salt
2 eggs, beaten
4–6 cups flour
6 cups oil
Butter

To make Honey Butter, stir 1 cup unsalted butter, softened, with ¼ cup honey. If you want a fluffy spread, mix it with an electric mixer on the highest speed for 10 minutes.

1. Place yeast, water, and sugar into a bowl. Let the yeast bubble for a couple of minutes.
2. Mix in the rest of the ingredients except the butter.
3. Knead the dough with clean hands until it is soft and not sticky. Add a little flour to the cough if it gets too sticky.
4. Place the dough back in the bowl and cover it with a clean towel. Let the dough rise in a warm place completely out of cold air drafts.
5. After the dough has doubled in size (this should take 30 minutes to an hour), sprinkle a little flour on a clean countertop, then rub a little pat of butter on your clean hands.
6. Gently stretch a small amount of dough (about the size of an egg) with your hands. Flatten it out into a circle or rectangle.
7. Meanwhile, ask an adult to heat the oil in a deep fryer.
8. Once the dough is shaped, ask the adult to carefully place one scone at a time into the fryer with tongs and cook it until it is golden brown.
9. As the scones finish cooking, drain them on paper towels.

Cowboy Cookies

These cookies aren't just your regular everyday chocolate chip cookies. They're filled with other ingredients like coconut, oats, and nuts that make them hearty enough for cowboys on the range. Granted, the cowboys out on the range wouldn't have had coconut, but this addition gives the cookies a modern twist.

Preparation Time: 15 minutes
Cooking Time: 10 to 12 minutes
Makes: About 2 dozen cookies

Ingredients

- 1 tablespoon butter, softened
- 1/2 cup sugar
- 1/2 cup brown sugar
- 1 egg
- 1 teaspoon vanilla
- 1 cup flour
- 1 teaspoon baking powder
- 1 teaspoon baking soda
- 1/4 teaspoon salt
- 1 teaspoon cinnamon
- 1 cup chocolate chips
- 1 cup oats
- 2/3 cup coconut
- 2/3 cup pecans

1. Preheat oven to 350F.
2. With an electric mixer, cream butter and sugars together.
3. Add eggs and vanilla; beat until smooth.
4. Add dry ingredients until completely blended.
5. Stir in remaining ingredients.

6. Roll dough into balls and place about an inch apart on a greased cookie sheet.
7. Bake for 10 to12 minutes.
8. Remove from pan with a spatula and let them cool on a cooling rack.

Jam Bars

The pioneers who settled the West preserved their fruit and vegetables in jars for use in the winter. They also made jams and jellies with them. These were not only spread on homemade bread and biscuits, but were also used in recipes, such as for these cookies.

Preparation Time: 15 minutes
Cooking Time: 35 minutes
Makes: 24 bar cookies

Ingredients

1½ cups flour
1 teaspoon baking powder
1 cup brown sugar
1½ cups quick cooking oats
¾ cup butter, softened
1 cup apricot jam (or any other
      kind of jam that you prefer)

1. Preheat oven to 350°F.
2. Mix the flour, baking powder, brown sugar, and oats together.
3. Add the butter and mix until the dough has a crumbly texture.
4. Pat half of the mixture into a greased 9 x 13-inch baking pan.
5. Spread with jam.
6. Cover with the rest of the crumb mixture.
7. Bake for 35 minutes.
8. Cool the bars, then cut.

47

Oh Henries

In 1920, a candy bar called Oh Henry!™ hit the market. It was made with peanuts, caramel, and fudge and was coated in chocolate. Trying to imitate the popular candy, someone developed a recipe for similar-tasting cookies and called them Oh Henries. Other people call these cookies Scotcheroos. Even though these originated in Chicago, they're a big hit out here in the West.

Ingredients

1 cup corn syrup
1 cup peanut butter
1 cup sugar
4–6 cups crisped rice
cereal
1 package (6 ounces)
milk chocolate
chips
1 package (6 ounces) butterscotch
chips

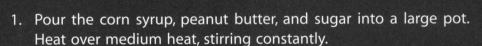

1. Pour the corn syrup, peanut butter, and sugar into a large pot. Heat over medium heat, stirring constantly.
2. When the sugar dissolves, remove the pan from the heat.
3. With a long-handled spoon, stir in crisped rice cereal until mixed completely.
4. Lightly coat a 9 x 13-inch pan with cooking spray.
5. Press cereal mixture into the pan with your clean hands. You may need to mist a little cooking spray on your hands to keep the cereal mixture from sticking to them.
6. Place milk chocolate chips and butterscotch chips into a microwave-safe bowl. Heat for 15 seconds in the microwave, stir,

Preparation Time: 5 minutes
Cooking Time: 10 to 12 minutes
    + 1 hour to cool
Serves: 15 to 18

heat for 15 more seconds, stir. Continue until the chips are completely melted.

7. With a spoon or butter knife, spread the melted chips evenly over the cookie layer.

8. Let the cookies cool approximately 1 hour before cutting into squares.

Peach Cobbler

In the fall, peaches are a popular fruit in the West. You can buy fresh-from-the-tree peaches at country farm stands and city farmers markets. People love eating peaches fresh, but they also like to cook them in pies and cobblers. Serve this cobbler plain or topped with vanilla ice cream.

Preparation Time: 15 minutes
Cooking Time: 50 minutes
Serves: 8 to 10

Ingredients

1 tablespoon butter
1 cup sugar
2 eggs, beaten
1 cup flour
2 teaspoons baking powder
1 cup milk
1 teaspoon vanilla
1 quart (32 ounces) sliced peaches, fresh or canned, including the juice

1. Preheat the oven to 350°F.
2. Place the butter in a 9 x 13-inch pan. Put the pan in the oven and leave it there until the butter melts.
3. Using oven mitts, carefully remove this pan from the oven and place it on top of the stove.
4. Mix the next six ingredients together in a bowl until it forms a smooth batter with no lumps.
5. Pour the batter into the pan of melted butter.
6. Carefully pour the peaches, with their juice, over the batter.
7. Bake for 50 minutes or until crust is golden brown.

Christmas Morning Citrus Drink

Oranges, lemons, and other citrus fruits grow well in the warm climates of the West. Since the harvesting season for navel oranges starts in late fall, this drink is perfect to serve at Christmas breakfast.

Preparation Time: 5 to 8 minutes
Serves: 20+

Ingredients

- 1 can (12 ounces) orange juice concentrate
- 1 can (12 ounces) lemonade concentrate
- 2 cups sugar
- 2 teaspoons vanilla extract
- 2 teaspoons almond extract
- 20 cups water

1. Pour all the ingredients into a large pot or punch bowl.
2. Stir completely.
3. Serve over ice.

Fourth of July
Homemade Root Beer

In the West, a favorite drink to serve for the Fourth of July is homemade root beer—made with a few simple ingredients inside a big water jug. This recipe requires the help of an adult, since dry ice can be dangerous.

Preparation Time: 5 minutes
Cooking Time: 15 to 20 minutes
Serves: 16

Ingredients

16 cups water
4 cups sugar
4 tablespoons root beer extract
2 cups ice cubes (approximately)
1½ pounds dry ice

1. Pour 8 cups of the water into a 2-gallon jug. Stir sugar into the water until the sugar is completely dissolved.
2. Add the root beer extract.
3. Stir in the ice cubes.
4. Add the rest of the water and stir.
5. Have an adult add the dry ice using gloves. NOTE: You cannot touch the dry ice with your bare skin. The dry ice is SO COLD that it will burn your skin.
6. VERY IMPORTANT: Leave the lid off the container. Watch as the dry ice billows steam out of the top of the jug. Because of the dry ice, it will be bubbly just like the root beer you buy in the store.
7. Let it steam for 15 to 20 minutes, then serve.

Halloween Chili

When I was a kid growing up in the West, we always had homemade chili and fresh bread on Halloween after we went trick-or-treating. This traditional fare warmed us up after our quest for candy on a cold autumn evening in our mountain home.

This chili can be served plain, topped with sour cream, or used with other recipes in this book, such as Navajo Tacos (see page 42) and Taquitos (see page 34).

Preparation Time: Overnight + 25 minutes
Cooking Time: 1½ hours
Serves: 4 to 6

Ingredients

- 1 cup dried kidney beans
- 1 pound ground beef or turkey
- 1 medium onion, chopped
- 1 large green pepper, chopped
- 1 can (16 ounces) crushed tomatoes
- 1 teaspoon salt
- 1 teaspoon pepper
- 1 teaspoon sugar
- 1 tablespoon chili powder

1. Rinse the kidney beans thoroughly. Pour them into a pot and cover them with water. Soak them overnight.
2. The next day, replace the water in the pot. Cook the beans for at least 1 hour on low heat, or until tender.
3. In a skillet, brown the ground meat with the onion and green pepper.
4. Drain off any grease.
5. Add tomatoes, salt, pepper, sugar, and chili powder.
6. Drain the water from the beans. Add them to the meat sauce.
7. Heat thoroughly.

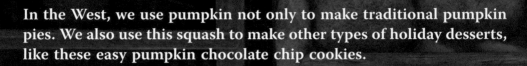

Thanksgiving Pumpkin Chocolate Chip Cookies

In the West, we use pumpkin not only to make traditional pumpkin pies. We also use this squash to make other types of holiday desserts, like these easy pumpkin chocolate chip cookies.

Preparation Time: 8 to 10 minutes
Cooking Time: 10 to 12 minutes
Makes: About 3 dozen cookies

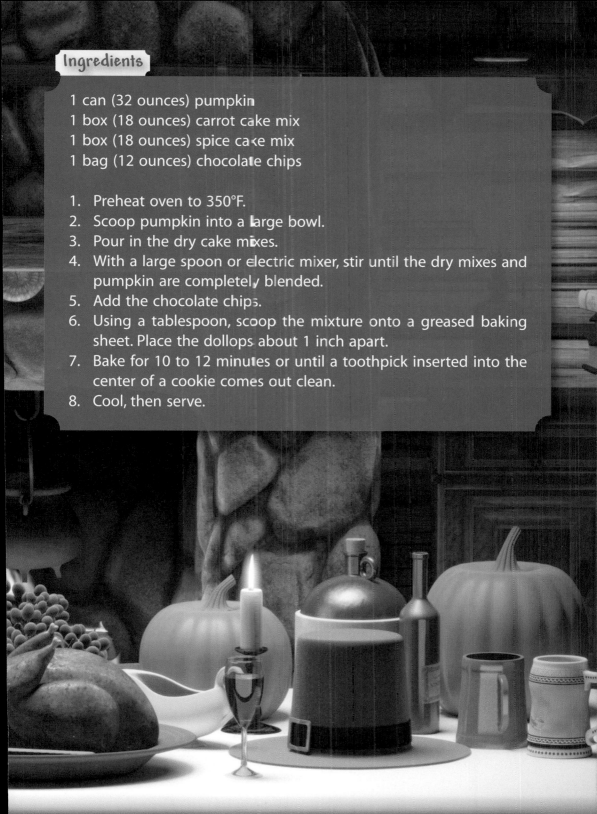

Ingredients

1 can (32 ounces) pumpkin
1 box (18 ounces) carrot cake mix
1 box (18 ounces) spice cake mix
1 bag (12 ounces) chocolate chips

1. Preheat oven to 350°F.
2. Scoop pumpkin into a large bowl.
3. Pour in the dry cake mixes.
4. With a large spoon or electric mixer, stir until the dry mixes and pumpkin are completely blended.
5. Add the chocolate chips.
6. Using a tablespoon, scoop the mixture onto a greased baking sheet. Place the dollops about 1 inch apart.
7. Bake for 10 to 12 minutes or until a toothpick inserted into the center of a cookie comes out clean.
8. Cool, then serve.

Books

Duffield, Katy S. *California History for Kids: Missions, Miners, and Moviemakers in the Golden State, Includes 21 Activities.* Chicago: Chicago Review Press, 2012.

Ichord, Loretta Frances. *Skillet Bread, Sourdough, and Vinegar Days: Cooking in Pioneer Days.* Minneapolis: Millbrook Press, 2005.

Radevsky, Anton. *The Wild West Pop-Up Book.* New York: Sterling, 2007.

Works Consulted

Cole's: Originators of the French Dip
http://213nightlife.com/colesfrenchdip

Cooks.com: California Salad
http://www.cooks.com/rec/doc/0,1943,157185-231193,00.html

Hawaiian Plate Lunch Macaroni Salad
http://www.squidoo.com/hawaiian-plate-lunch-macaroni-salad?utm_source=google&utm_medium=imgres&utm_campaign=framebuster

Lindsey, Robert. "California Grows Her Own Cuisine." *The New York Times*, August 18, 1985. http://www.nytimes.com/1985/08/18/travel/california-grows-her-own-cuisine.html?pagewanted=1

Nelson, Paul. "The Creators of Fry Sauce Turn 60." Ksl.com, March 10, 2010. http://www.ksl.com/?nid=148&sid=9958589

The Official Santa Maria Style Barbecue Site
http://santamariavalleybbq.com/

Paiva, Derk. "How to Make Hawaii Plate-lunch-style Macaroni Salad." *Hawaii Magazine*, December 4, 2009. http://www.hawaiimagazine.com/blogs/hawaii_today/2009/12/4/hawaii_style_plate_lunch_macaroni_salad_recipe/3

Philippe's: History
http://www.philippes.com/history/

Sourdough Home: An Exploration of Sourdough
http://www.sourdoughhome.com/

Steinhauer, Jennifer. "Carbo-Loading, Hawaiian Style." *The New York Times*, November 12, 2008. http://www.nytimes.com/2008/11/12/dining/12plate.html?_r=1

What's Cooking America
http://whatscookingamerica.net/

Further Reading

On the Internet

Alan's Kitchen: Cowboy and Western Recipes
http://www.alanskitchen.com/Cowboy/default.htm

California Harvest Calendar
http://www.pickyourown.org/CAharvestcalendar.htm

Cowboy's Western Recipes
http://www.cowboyshowcase.com/recipes.htm

Legends of America: Old West Recipes
http://www.legendsofamerica.com/we-oldwestrecipes.html

Western American Cooking: Far West Region
http://whatscookingamerica.net/AmericanRegionalFoods/FarWest.htm

The Wild West: Native American Recipes
http://www.thewildwest.org/nativeamericans/nativeamericanrecipes

1519	Cortés lands in Mexico and defeats Aztecs.
1769	Juniper Serra founds the first of 21 missions in California.
1803	The Louisiana Purchase sparks westward expansion.
1847	Sourdough starter is brought to San Francisco over the Oregon Trail. The first Chinese immigrants settle in San Francisco.
1849	Gold is discovered in the Sierra Nevada, prompting the California gold rush.
1850	California becomes the 31st state in the United States.
1869	The final spike is driven to complete the first Transcontinental Railroad at Promontory Point, Utah.
1890	Idaho becomes a state.
1896	Utah becomes a state.
1908	Cole's, a restaurant in Los Angeles, opens; later, it will claim to have invented the French-dipped sandwich.
1918	Philippe Mathieu, owner of Philippe's Restaurant in Southern California, claims he has invented the French-dipped sandwich.
1931	The Santa Maria Club holds its first Stag Barbecue, which popularizes Santa Maria Style Barbecue.
1937	Bob Cobb, owner of The Brown Derby in Hollywood, invents the Cobb salad.
1940s	Chef Don Carlos Edwards invents fry sauce at Don Carlos Barbecue, which will become the Arctic Circle restaurant in Salt Lake City, Utah.
1940	Ralph Pesqueria invents taquitos ("little tacos") at the El Indio Restaurant in San Diego.
1946	Glen Bell, a World War II veteran, opens a hot dog stand in San Bernardino, California; it will become the Taco Bell franchise.
1948	Dick and Mac McDonald open the first McDonald's restaurant in San Bernardino.
1951	Robert O. Peterson opens the first Jack in the Box restaurant in San Diego; his menu features sandwiches on sourdough bread.
1957	In New York City, Moto Saito opens the first U.S. sushi restaurant, starting a trend that leads to the California roll.
1959	Alaska and Hawaii become the 49th and 50th states.
1970s	Cooks across California begin experimenting with fusion cooking, blending recipes from different countries and using fresh, locally grown ingredients and simple preparation methods; this style becomes known as California cuisine.
1980	Ed LaDou (the Prince of Pizza) at Spago in Western Hollywood and pizza chefs at the Chez Panisse café in Berkeley, California, invent California-style pizza.
1985	Working for Wolfgang Puck's California Pizza Kitchen, LaDou invents barbecued chicken pizza.
2011	The original 1847 San Francisco sourdough starter continues to be used to make sourdough bread.

Index

About the
AUTHOR

Author Amie Jane Leavitt (back) and her nieces and nephews from left to right: Ava, Isaac, Cameron, Adda, and Colby

Author and photographer Amie Jane Leavitt is also a baker and a cook. She makes all sorts of things in her kitchen ranging from salsa and jams to delectable desserts and tasty entrées. Since she grew up in the American West and has lived in this region for most of her life, she has an in-depth personal knowledge of this area's unique cuisine. Along with this cookbook for Mitchell Lane Publishers, she also wrote and took the photographs for Kids Can Cook: *Southwestern Recipes*. Leavitt is the author of more than 40 books and has also had her work published in magazines and national school assessments. Find out more about her at http://www.amiejaneleavitt.com.